Seven Winning Strategies

Seven Winning Strategies

To Help Your Children <u>Succeed</u> In School and Life

Bill Cecil

Best Year Ever! Press
Mason, Michigan

Seven Winning Strategies
To Help Your Children
<u>Succeed</u> In School and Life
by Bill Cecil

Published by:
Best Year Ever! Press
Mason, MI 48854
Phone: 517-244-0465
Email: BillCecil@BestYearEver.net
Website: BestYearEver.net

All rights reserved. No part of this book may be reproduced or transmitted in any form or by any means, electronic or mechanical, including photocopying, recording, or by any information storage and retrieval system, without written permission from the author, except for the inclusion of brief quotations in reviews.

Copyright © 2020 by Bill Cecil

ISBN-13: 978-0-9779411-1-7

Library of Congress Control Number: 2020907023

First Edition. Printed in the United States of America

Page Design by One On One Book Production,
West Hills, California

Cover Design by Robert Aulicino, Prescott, Arizona

Cartoon: Copyright © Genildo Ronchi, used by permission.

Dedicated to...

Those parents/guardians
striving to be the best role models,
teachers, and coaches they can be
to their children!

Thanks to...

Shana Barnum, Chris Salmon, Vickie Tisdale, and my wonderful wife, Andrea, for all your valuable input, ideas, and encouragement throughout the writing of this book. Each of you played a significant role in helping me make this book something I feel confident and really excited to share with others.

Also, a special thanks to my mom and dad
for being the inspiration behind this book
by instilling each of these seven winning strategies
into all five of their children!

CONTENTS

Preface	ix
Introduction	1
WINNING STRATEGY 1: Adopt and Develop a Growth Mindset	7
WINNING STRATEGY 2: Strive to Make Every Year Your Best Year Ever!	15
WINNING STRATEGY 3: Attendance: Show Up On A Regular Basis	21
WINNING STRATEGY 4: Attitude: Think Positive! Be Positive! Believe You Can Achieve!	27
WINNING STRATEGY 5: Effort: Try, Work Hard, and Don't Give Up!	35
WINNING STRATEGY 6: Become a Goal Setter and Goal-Getter by Following These Six Steps	43
WINNING STRATEGY 7: Consistently Use a Team Approach and Strive to Become a Strong Team Player	53
Closing Thoughts	63
Message to Schools, School Districts, PTO/PTA	65
Message to Local Businesses and Other Potential Sponsors	67

viii

PREFACE

"I believe in you." ~Charlie Brown

I want to take a moment to let you know why I wrote this book and why I think it is worth reading. For years, I have kept a small Charlie Brown stuffed toy in my office to remind me that *your past doesn't equal your future,* and to remind me of my mission/purpose to help others remember that as well...Let me explain.

Growing up as a middle child of five, I wanted to be more confident and successful like Snoopy from the comic strip *Peanuts*. However, I seemed to be more like Charlie Brown. Just in case you don't know 'Chuck' as closely as I do, here is a brief description from *Wikipedia*:

> *"Charlie Brown is a meek, kind, innocent, gentle-hearted character with many anxieties, and is depicted as being shy. He is a child possessed with significant determination and hope but often fails due to his insecurities."*

Despite having great parents that loved me very much, for whatever reason, I had bouts with low self-confidence and other anxieties as a young child. Like the black zigzag design on Charlie Brown's yellow shirt, my life seemed to have many ups and downs caused by my negative thinking, low self-esteem, and poor behavior that were causing me to struggle – especially at school.

However, I was very fortunate and blessed to have parents (and many teachers and coaches) that never gave up on me and continued to work with me – trying to get me to change my thinking and to learn to believe in myself. With time and lots of patience, the seeds they planted finally started to take root and began growing in my mind. Over time, my attitude, thinking, and belief in myself started to soar, and my life began to change dramatically for the better – unlike my friend Charlie Brown.

When I became a teacher, it didn't take long for me to realize that there are a lot of other Charlie Browns out there in the world – some that sat in my classroom each year – struggling like I did when I was a kid. This is when I discovered my purpose as a teacher. I decided to make it my mission to **uplift**, **motivate**, and **get my students to believe in themselves.** Not only did this become my mission, it became my passion!

I started reading many books and studying about this topic sparking a lifelong obsession. I wanted to learn as much as I could about this subject to better help my students (and eventually other educators and teachers) by teaching them how to use the **seven winning strategies** that I have included in this book.

After retiring from the classroom, my dad encouraged me to reach out to "parents" to share these strategies. He convinced me about the *even more powerful impact* these strategies will have on children if they are given the opportunity to learn about them and practice using them *both* at home and school!

Whether you are raising a Charlie Brown, Snoopy, Linus, Lucy, Pig-pen, Peppermint Patty, Franklin, or even a Woodstock in your family, I <u>KNOW</u> (from experience) they will greatly benefit from learning to master these seven winnings strategies and turning them into *success habits* that will help them succeed every year in school and throughout their lives.

So, as you prepare to read and use this powerful little book with your children, I want you to know that (just like what Charlie Brown once said to Snoopy in one of the early *Peanuts'* comics)…**I believe in you!**

Introduction

"Anyone who does anything to help a child in life is a hero to me." ~Mr. Rogers

The purpose of this powerful little book is to provide you with seven winning strategies that you can use to help your children succeed and flourish every year in school and throughout their lives. These strategies work like magic!

However, they **are not** magic! These strategies **only** work as long as your children consistently 'work' the strategies. Therefore, your key role (working together with your children's schools) is to *teach*, *model*, and *practice* using the strategies with your children throughout the entire school year – praising and encouraging them whenever you see one of these strategies being used.

The goal is for your children to use these winning strategies long enough so that they become *Success Habits* for life.

Before I jump into the seven winning strategies, I want to take a moment and give you a quick overview of why I believe this little book is worth investing some of your valuable family time and energy. If your children master these strategies and turn them into successful habits, they will pay big dividends throughout their schooling and beyond. I also want to share with you four things you can do to greatly increase your children's success in mastering these seven strategies.

Overview
"Change your thoughts and you change your world."
~Norman Vincent Peale
Author of The Power of Positive Thinking

Dr. Peale's quote above provides the perfect overview and focus for this book and the reason it is well worth your time and energy to help your children develop the power of positive, purposeful thinking. **How you think** and **what you think** plays a significant role in shaping your *reality*. Your thoughts and beliefs act as a strong magnet attracting more of what you think about, focus on, and what you expect to happen in your world.

Better yet, think of your world as a garden and your thoughts as the seeds you will plant in your garden. Successful gardeners, take time to think about what they want to grow and then deliberately plant only those seeds knowing that if you plant weeds you will get weeds, and if you plant flowers you will get flowers!

Once the seeds are planted, the gardener provides the proper amount of water, light, and plant food (belief in self, positive thinking, and other empowering mindsets) to help those seeds take root and grow into strong, healthy plants. Also, during this time, they will continually weed their garden of any unwanted plants (self-doubt, negative thinking, and other debilitating mindsets) which will interfere with the plants they are trying to grow.

Therefore, the focus of this powerful little book is designed to help you help your children learn that they truly have the power to *change their world* (at school and beyond) by *changing their thoughts, beliefs*, and *expectations* to better match what they want to attract more of in their lives – IF they are willing to work and keep working until they get the results they want.

Introduction

Next, to ensure getting maximum results from using the seven winning strategies in this book, I have provided you with a foolproof game plan that will guarantee you and your children amazing results!

The Winning Game Plan To Get The Most Out Of This Book

For each of the seven winning strategies, I will provide you with a brief *Strategy Overview* (🔍) of what the strategy is and how it can become a successful habit that will help your children succeed in school (and other areas of their lives) each year. I will also provide *Strategy Talking Points* (💬) which will include some key talking points/conversation starters or sample conversations you can use to help introduce, explain, and talk <u>with</u> your children about each strategy. Finally, I will include with each winning strategy *IDEAS/ACTIVITIES* (🏃) you can use to help model and practice the strategy being introduced with your children. *Be sure to modify and adjust the information and ideas shared to best fit each child's age, learning level, and individual interests and needs.*

Again, make sure you take time to praise and encourage your children as they start to use these seven strategies. This will help motivate them to keep using the strategies long enough to start seeing and feeling positive results. Finally, in order to ensure these strategies work, you must commit to consistently doing four things throughout the entire school year with your children.

They are:

1. You Must Model the Way

"Children are great imitators, so give them something great to imitate." ~Anonymous

Seven Winning Strategies

As your children's primary role model, you must lead by example. Hopefully, grandparents, aunts, uncles, teachers, coaches, clergy – everyone who might have influence – will be positive role models in their lives as well. But make no bones about it, **YOU are your children's primary and most influential role model, teacher and coach!**

Therefore, it will be essential for you to consistently model (if you aren't already) the strategies and skills covered in this book which you will be asking your children to learn and master. You **MUST model a "do-as-I-do" approach**, rather than a "do-as-I-say" approach for getting maximum results.

2. Make Time Each Day to Talk With (Not Just To) Your Children

"What will your children remember?
Moments spent listening, talking, playing and sharing together may be the most important times of all."
~*Gloria Gaither*

As you set out this school year to teach, model, and practice using the seven winning strategies with your children, I encourage you to take this opportunity (if you haven't already) to start building a very special bond with them. They should always feel comfortable coming to you whenever they need someone to talk with and confide in. You want your children to see you as that trusted person who they can share their hopes, dreams, and concerns with – knowing you will be there to listen to them, comfort and encourage them, and help them solve any challenges that they will face.

This doesn't just happen. This is something you must invest a lot of time and energy in order to help build that trust and special bond with them. Here are two great ways to help make this happen. Open up and talk <u>with</u> (not at) your children, and be sure to give them your undivided attention when they are speaking to you. It's that easy! Just get in the habit of talking with and listening to your children each day. This will allow your children to learn more about you...and you more about them.

Take time to discuss and talk about the main ideas included in each of the seven winning strategies. This will provide you with plenty of conversation starters and talking points (◯) to talk about with your children each day. Remember, when it comes to talking about school and the winning strategies, the goal will be to create uplifting, empowering conversations between your children and yourself instead of lecturing them about what they should and should not be doing.

3. Embrace the *Highlights* Magazine's Mission Statement: "Fun with a Purpose"

"The more fun you have, the better you will perform. The better you perform, the more fun you will have."
~Jim Afremow, Ph.D., Author of The Champion's Mind

Studies show that happy workers tend to be more successful!

This is why it is so important that you help your children adopt a "fun with a purpose" attitude about going to school this year. To help make this happen, you **MUST model the proper attitude and mindset that this is going to be a fun and exciting school year.**

The enthusiasm, excitement, and joy that you show towards your children's schooling (exciting things they are doing and new things they are learning) throughout the year will surely begin to rub off on them, and they will start carrying more enthusiasm, excitement, and joy into school with them each day. This will have a powerful impact on helping your children have more fun at school, thus leading to more success.

Seven Winning Strategies

By the way, not only will the "fun with a purpose" approach benefit your children in school but will also carry over into many other areas in their lives as well – like home life, playing sports, participating in activities, working at part-time jobs, and eventually life as an adult.

4. You Must Apply the 21/90 Rule: "It Takes 21 Days to Form a Habit and 90 Days to Create a Lifestyle"

"First we form habits. Then they form us." ~Jim Rohn

It usually takes twenty-one days to form or break a habit. Most diet and exercise programs work as long as people begin seeing positive results. This takes about twenty-one to thirty days. Unfortunately, this is why many of those same diet and exercise programs fail, because the people using them expect instant results and quit too soon.

Therefore, it will be essential that you help your children stick with each of the seven powerful strategies in this little book long enough to start seeing positive results. This will encourage them to keep using the strategies long enough to turn them into successful habits creating a lifestyle that will enable your children to excel in school and many other areas in their lives.

★★★★★

That's it! If you follow this winning game plan and commit to doing the four things mentioned above consistently throughout the year, you will be able to help your children create *success habits* that will help them succeed every year in school and beyond!

So, do I have your commitment? Or, more importantly, do your children have your commitment?!!

If so, CONGRATULATIONS!!! Read on, and let's start creating some <u>real</u> magic!

Winning Strategy 1
Adopt and Develop a Growth Mindset

"Whether you <u>think you can</u>, or you <u>think you can't</u> – you're right."
~Henry Ford

> *A mindset is an attitude, belief, or expectation a person (or group of people) has that drives the way they think and act.*

One of the most important things you can do to help your children excel in school (and in life) is to help them embrace and develop as many healthy, empowering mindsets as possible – such as a **growth mindset** and a **positive mindset**. Like soil to seeds in a garden, these mindsets will support and provide the needed nutrients to help your children grow the winning strategies introduced in this book into strong *success habits*.

Let's start with the importance of helping your children adopt and develop a *growth mindset*.

People with a <u>growth mindset</u> believe they can always learn more and do anything they set their mind to do with the right amount of time, effort, and patience! People with a growth mindset often get excited to try new things, see challenges as opportunities for growth and don't stress out too much over mistakes made. They know they can learn from them to help prepare for future success. Each success they experience will help to validate and strengthen the belief and mindset that they *CAN*!

The opposite of a growth mindset is a *fixed mindset*. Adopting a _fixed mindset_ is a recipe for failure. People that live by a fixed mindset tend to believe they were born with only so much intelligence, talents and skills. They believe they are either naturally good at certain things or they are not. If they aren't, they often believe there is nothing they can do to improve (or acquire new skills) in those areas. They quit trying too soon, or worse, don't even try – validating the belief that they *CAN'T*!

The key goal for you is to help your children develop the habit of thinking they *CAN* rather than thinking they *CAN'T*. This is essential because whichever mindset your children thinks/believes becomes a self-fulfilling prophecy which will affect the actions they take (or don't take) leading to results that match their thoughts and beliefs.

Use the following talking points/conversation starters to help introduce your children to the importance of adopting and developing a strong growth mindset:

- Read the quote from Henry Ford at the beginning of this section to your children. Then, ask them what they think it means. Once they have shared their thoughts, use the quote to help introduce and explain the difference between a **growth mindset** (a think-you-can attitude) and a *fixed mindset* (a think-you-can't attitude) that influences the way people think and act.

- Explain to your children that our brains are very powerful. They are so powerful because what we believe, think, and expect to happen (all things we do with our brains) play a huge part in what we are able to do and accomplish throughout our lives.

- Share with your children some examples from your own life when a growth mindset helped you accomplish or do some special things – also times where a fixed mindset held you back from being successful. Be sure to use examples that focus more on "effort" than "talent" to help plant the seeds that a *strong desire*, *belief in self* and *giving effort* play a significant role in many of our successful outcomes.

- Ask your children to share some examples from their lives where a growth mindset helped them to accomplish or do some special things and an example or two where a negative mindset held them back from being successful. If your children are unable to think of any, share some examples from your children as they were growing up, highlighting positive examples. Again, focus more on "effort" than "talent" to help plant the seeds that desire, belief in self, and effort play a key part in many of our successes.

- Let your children know that your goal is to help them get in the habit of thinking "I CAN" (by adopting a growth mindset) more often than thinking "I CAN'T" (by refusing to adopt a fixed mindset) to help maximize their opportunities to excel in school – and in other areas of their lives outside of school.

Note: To help you achieve this goal with your children, I am giving you five **IDEAS/ACTIVITIES** (🏃) you can start using to help your children develop a strong growth mindset and an empowering "I CAN" attitude.

🏃**1**: Listen closely to how you speak <u>around</u> your children and how your children speak <u>around</u> you. Listen for

Seven Winning Strategies

growth-mindset and fixed-mindset statements. When you hear yourself or your children using a fixed-mindset statement, stop and immediately "pull that weed" by changing the statement into a growth-mindset statement. For example, change statements like "I can't" to **"I can!"**…"It's impossible" to **"I'll find a way!"**…"I'm not smart enough" to **"I will learn how to do this!"**…"I failed" to **"Mistakes help me learn!"**…"I give up" to **"I will keep trying until I get this!"**

Another possible way to approach this with your children is to turn it into a game. This can get you all in the habit of listening closely to each other. When another person in your family uses a fixed-mindset or negative statement, you stop them and make them change it into a growth-mindset or positive statement.

For example, if you hear any of your children say, *"I don't have any friends at school,"* you will stop them and say, *"That's a negative. Change it to a positive."* Then, they would have to stop, think for a moment, and re-word their statement to sound more positive like, *"I am going to start working to make more friends at school this year."*

By turning this into a game, this activity becomes more fun and doesn't sound like you are correcting them while you are trying to get your children in the habit of using more empowering speech. Plus, it will work on their listening skills because your children will love to catch you when you slip up using a fixed-mindset or negative comment. They can stop you by saying, *"That's a negative. Change it to a positive."*

🏃2: Place some growth-mindset statements around the house in highly visible areas (bathroom mirrors, refrigerator, door frames, etc.) where you and your children can see and use them often until they become a habit. This will help to drive everyone's thoughts, beliefs, and actions every day.

Note: You can Google "growth-mindset vocabulary" to find more examples.

🏃3: Train your ears to start listening for growth-mindset statements. Praise your children every time you hear them being used. It will motivate your children to use them more often (especially around you) increasing the odds of this becoming a habit that will drive positive thoughts, beliefs, and actions more and more each day.

🏃4: **Avoid making** fixed-mindset statements about yourself to your children. For example, don't ever share that you struggled with certain subjects/skills in school or in activities outside of school because you were not smart or talented enough. **Statements like:** *"I was never good at doing Math. My brain wasn't wired that way,"* or *"I can't draw, sing, or act because I wasn't born with a creative bone in my body."*

More importantly, don't ever make a fixed-mindset statement about your children – especially about how you are afraid they may have inherited some of the same struggles from you or that they have just never been good at certain things. **Statements like:** *"Don't blame yourself for not being good at spelling. You must have gotten that from me because I have always been a lousy speller,"* or *"You've never been really good at basketball, so maybe you should find another sport to play."*

Finally, never let fixed-mindset statements your children make about themselves go unchallenged. **Statements like:** *"I can't learn to play an instrument,"* or *"I'm not smart like the other kids."*

Powerful, destructive statements like these can be very damaging for several reasons:

- They plant seeds in your children's minds that because you struggled they will likely struggle in these areas as well.

Seven Winning Strategies

- They only reinforce your children's beliefs that if they ever struggle with something, it will always be a struggle.
- Fixed-mindset statements like these may cause them to give little or no effort in these areas because they already believe they *can't* so why even try, or they feel they don't have to try because you don't expect much from them anyway – thus holding them back from reaching their full potential.
- If children believe that you have low expectations for them and/or you don't challenge their low expectations, it could lower their own self-worth.

Remember, your goal is to help them adopt and develop a strong, growth mindset by continually planting positive, powerful seeds in their minds. Tell them you believe they can accomplish anything they set their mind to and are willing to work at it long enough to make it happen. Get them in the habit of believing they can do it as well. The next activity will give you plenty of opportunities to do just that!

🏃5: Be like Mr. Rogers, and look for different ways to promote and practice using a growth mindset around your children and provide them with ample opportunities to do the same. Fred Rodgers (the beloved host of *Mr. Rogers' Neighborhood* – which aired on PBS for over 31 seasons) never hesitated to accept an invitation from his many guests to participate in an activity that they came on the show to share with his home audience – from playing many different musical instruments, learning new dances, doing different arts and crafts projects, and even learning sign language to communicate with a gorilla.

Mr. Rogers would embrace each new learning opportunity with joy and passion – despite the many struggles, missteps, and flubs you would expect someone to make while learning something for the very first time. This didn't seem to bother him. In fact, he would purposely leave unflattering footage of his many bloopers in the show. He wanted to send a powerful message to the children watching his show about the importance of having fun and not worrying about making mistakes – especially when learning new things. This is the same message you want to send to your children.

Whenever your children invite you to play a new board game, video game or participate in a new activity that you haven't done in the past, be like Mr. Rogers and jump in with both feet modeling to them that you are willing to learn new things and can have a lot of fun while learning. You can also show an interest in wanting to learn more about what they are learning in school. This will give them the opportunity to play the role of the teacher, while giving you plenty of opportunities to learn side-by-side with your children – modeling how to approach new challenges with an "I CAN!" attitude.

Also, get in the habit of asking your children if they would like the opportunity to help you out with things you are working on around the house – especially when it will involve them learning something new like how to use a specific tool, appliance, or involve learning a new skill like baking, painting, repairing something, etc. Focus more on making the experience fun for them rather than on the final outcome having to be perfect. You can also do this with hobbies that you enjoy doing!

Finally, if your children ever ask if they can help you with something that you are doing, if at all possible, gladly accept their invitation. Use each opportunity to show them that working with you is not only a lot of fun, it is increasing their desire to try new things and their love of learning. This will help to build their "I CAN" growth mindsets.

Seven Winning Strategies

Winning Strategy 2

Strive to Make Every Year Your Best Year Ever!

"Where there is no vision, there is no hope."
~George Washington Carver

"If you want to be happy, set a goal that commands your thoughts, liberates your energy, and inspires your hopes." ~Andrew Carnegie

"It's all about the journey, not the outcome." ~Carl Lewis

Regardless of the fact that your children already love going to school, hate going to school, or are somewhere in between, you now need to help create a big, exciting vision/goal that will **"command their thoughts," "liberate their energy,"** and **"inspire their hopes"** throughout the entire upcoming school year – *especially* if they have not enjoyed going in the past!

This will be your opportunity to start planting the *seeds of success* in your children's minds about the new school year. Start by explaining how excited you are about this school year because you already expect it to be something really special – their *Best Year Ever!* Let your children know you plan to work closely with them to help make it happen!

It will be important to stress that *Best Year Ever!* doesn't mean *Perfect Year Ever!* or *Challenge Free Year Ever!* Rather, ***Best***

Seven Winning Strategies

Year Ever! is a powerful approach (mindset) to live your life by. It is a combination of having a ***positive-growth mindset*** and ***high expectations*** so that no matter what life throws at you, you will make the most out of your current situation, and always look for new ways to improve and grow in order to become the best you can be! It's <u>not</u> about trying to be perfect. It's about learning to dream big dreams and striving to grasp them. ***Best Year Ever!*** is about getting in the habit of trying to reach a little higher and push yourself a little more each day to reach new levels within yourself. **It's about learning to expect the best and working to get your best!** This is what you want to convince your children to do, this year and all those that follow!

Finally, it's vital that you help your children understand that *Best Year Ever!* **is about learning to enjoy the journey rather than waiting for the final outcome at the end of the school year before they can finally celebrate and be happy.** Your children working daily to have their *Best Year Ever!* should be celebrated and enjoyed <u>each</u> day, because they will be working to accomplish something truly special other than just trying to get through the year. Your children will be working to create *success habits* to make every year in school (and beyond) their *Best Year Ever!*

By now, you may be thinking, this sounds great, but how do I begin?

Note: Following is a sample conversation you can use to help introduce the ***Best Year Ever!*** mindset/vision/goal with your children. DO NOT try to memorize or have this exact conversation with your children. Pull out some key talking points that you can use with them.

Winning Strategy 2

PART ONE: THE OFFER

"Imagine that a person comes up to you and offers to help you make this school year your best year ever! A year that you will never forget. A year that will include lots of good times, exciting challenges, tremendous growth, and fond memories. It will be a school year that you will enjoy so much it will seem to fly by, and at its end, you will look back and say, 'Wow! What a year!' I'm asking you, is this the type of school year you would be interested in having?"

Pause a moment to let your children respond and then say:

"Well, today is your lucky day because I'm that person, and I'm offering to you – right now – an opportunity to make this upcoming school year (and every year) your best year ever!

"I'll help give you a school year you'll never forget. If you've had great years in the past, that's wonderful. Then this will be another great year you can add to the list.

"However, if for some reason, you haven't really enjoyed school in the past this is your lucky day because this will be the year your feelings about school will change. I am that confident in my ability to help you make this year very special. I know in my heart that I can help you make it your best year ever.

"IF…"

PART TWO: THE CATCH

Pay extra close attention to "THE CATCH." It will introduce the powerful three-word-success formula (Winning Strategies 3-5) you will be asking your children to *commit to doing* the entire school year. Mastering this three-word-success formula will not only help your children make every year in school their ***Best Year Ever!*** but will help them excel outside the classroom as well. The three words that will be introduced in this section are three of the top things that employees have control over that will either help them thrive in the workplace or get them fired depending on how well they have mastered them.

Continue the *Best Year Ever!* mindset/vision/goal sample conversation:

> *"If?...I know what you are probably thinking right now. 'I knew it sounded too good to be true – best year ever. There's always a catch! Nothing in this world is free. Am I right?'*
>
> *"Well, you are right. There is a catch! In order to have your best year ever, you must promise or commit to doing three things for me this year.*
>
> *"That's it! Just three things!*
>
> *"The good news is that these three things you must promise to do are easy to learn and easy to do. However, you **must** do all three to be successful. You can't choose your two favorites and leave one out. All three things must be done – and done well to have your best year ever.*
>
> *"I can guarantee you that you'll have your best year ever if you learn and practice these three things – three words – consistently all year long...**Guaranteed!***
>
> *"So listen very carefully because the next three words I say are going to enable you to have your best year ever. They are **Attendance...Attitude...Effort!***
>
> *"That's it! Attendance, attitude, and effort.*
>
> *"That's the catch. All you have to do is learn and practice using these three words on a daily basis, and I'm confident that at the end of the year you will be able to look back and say, 'That was my best year ever!'*
>
> *"Now, before I ask you to commit to these three words, I want to quickly go over each one with you to make sure we have the same understanding of what it means and what I expect to see you doing this year to have your best year ever."*

Note: This ***Best Year Ever!*** sample conversation will be continued in the Winning Strategies 3-5.

Winning Strategy 2

🚶6: You may want to write the three words – Attendance, Attitude, Effort – on some note cards, poster board, or blank pieces of paper that you can post somewhere highly visible in your home. For instance, place them in your children's bedrooms or on the refrigerator so you can refer to them often throughout the year.

Seven Winning Strategies

Winning Strategy 3
Attendance: Show Up On A Regular Basis

"You miss 100% of the shots you don't take." ~*Wayne Gretzky*

The first step to success is showing up! Your children will not have a good *shot* at being successful at anything if they don't show up and keep showing up on a regular basis. **Studies have shown that students who attend school regularly tend to perform better academically, get better grades, and enjoy going to school.** This makes sense because there are many advantages your children will experience by showing up on a regular basis. Here are just a few of them:

- More opportunities to learn the subject matter and skills being taught as well as more opportunities to practice using the vital learning strategies that are designed to help make learning and completing assigned work easier.

- Less anxiety trying to figure out what was missed while being absent.

- Less stress trying to complete new assignments as well as the work missed while being gone.

- More opportunities to bond and feel connected with teacher(s) and classmates.

Seven Winning Strategies

Remember, the more days your children attend school, the more *shots* they'll have to make this school year their *Best Year Ever!* Therefore, be sure you stress the importance of having great attendance this year in order to help make that happen!

Below is the continuation of the *Best Year Ever!* conversation **focusing on Attendance** – the first word in the three-word-success formula you want your children to master this year. Again, please don't feel you have to try and memorize and deliver this exact conversation. Use this to pull out key talking points you want to share with your children when discussing the importance of working to have good attendance during the school year.

Attendance

"The first word you must learn and master this year in order to have your best year ever is ATTENDANCE. Of the three words or things to do, this is probably the easiest. All you have to do is go to class. That's it – just show up!

"You have to have good attendance this year. You have to go to school on a regular basis to put yourself in a position to have your best year ever. You can't possibly have your best year ever if you don't show up. Think about it. Michael Jordan **(or choose any other successful athlete, celebrity, person from history, etc.),** *without a doubt one of the greatest basketball players/athletes of all time, could never have helped lead the Chicago Bulls to winning six NBA championships if he just sat in the locker room all the time bragging about how good he was. First, he had to consistently step out onto the basketball court throughout the season to have any hope of having his best year ever each year. You have to do the same thing by going to school on a regular basis to give yourself this chance.*

Winning Strategy 3

"Another reason it's so important to show up on a consistent basis is so you don't fall behind or feel out of sync with the rest of the class.

"The more you miss, the harder it will be to feel a part of the group because each time you go back to school after being absent, your classmates won't be in the same place they were when you left. Life will have gone on while you were home sitting on the couch playing video games. Plus, when you return to school, you will have to work extra hard to make up all the work you missed in addition to completing any new work you are being assigned. Just think, you can avoid all this unnecessary stress and anxiety by consistently going to class. It's that simple.

"As important as attendance is, I want you to know that I understand there will most likely be a few times you may need to miss school because you're really sick or have a doctor's appointment. That's okay. However, I'm asking you to do the best you can to show up to school this year on a regular basis. In fact, I want you to challenge yourself this year to break your own personal record for the least number of absences in one year. Shoot for your best record! And if you've had a year(s) with perfect attendance, try to match that record again!

"Do you have any questions about attendance? Then let's move on to the second word you need to learn and do in order to have your best year ever." **(To be continued)**

Note: Following are Two **IDEAS/ACTIVITIES** Designed To Help Your Children Have Strong Attendance:

🏃7: Depending on each child's attendance record, I have provided two different options that you can use to help motivate your children to go to school on a regular basis and reap the many rewards that come with having great attendance.

Seven Winning Strategies

Option A: Provide an incentive which your children can earn to beat or tie their best attendance record from previous school years. If you can't remember how many days each of your children have missed in the past, you can look at old report cards or just set an arbitrary number like five (or less) days for the entire school year for them to earn the incentive. You can also include smaller incentives each month for perfect attendance. This will help to keep them motivated throughout the entire year. To get better *buy-in* from your children, have them work with you to decide on the attendance incentive(s) that can be earned this year.

Option B: If any of your children have really struggled with poor attendance (or chronic tardiness) in the past, this may be a more realistic **IDEA/ACTIVITY** to start with. Instead of setting a year-long goal or monthly goals to shoot for, you can set it up where they can earn a smaller incentive – if they can reach a certain number of days in a row without missing school or being tardy. Each time they reach that goal and earn their incentive, you can create a new goal increasing the number of days in a row and provide a new incentive for them to try to earn.

To help keep your children motivated working on this **IDEA/ACTIVITY**, keep track of the number of days in a row each child doesn't miss school or isn't tardy on a calendar or next to the word "Attendance" you posted somewhere in your home for them to see – like displaying their scores on a scoreboard. Be sure to also post the set number of days each child has to reach in order to earn their incentive. This way they are constantly reminded of the target they are trying to hit.

Winning Strategy 3

🚶8: Here is a strategy you can use with your children that will not only help with attendance and being on time each day, but it will also help all of you have a more relaxed start to each school morning. The goal of this activity is to help your children get organized and have everything they will need for school the next day already in place before they go to bed each night. This will help prevent them from running around frantically in the morning trying to find what they need.

It will be important to assign each child a specific place in your home for the school year which will be their spot to put everything needed for school the next day. This should be done before they sit down to relax each evening or before they go to bed. Things to put in this spot should include completed homework, lunch money, musical instruments, signed notes and permission slips, backpacks, jackets, hats, gloves, boots, etc.

Create a procedure where each night you will meet one-on-one with your children for a few minutes to double-check that everything needed is already in place for the next morning. Besides taking this nightly opportunity to make sure everything is organized, it's an ideal time to check in with them by asking questions about their day – letting them share some of their highs and lows. This is also a perfect time to let each child know how excited and proud you are about how hard they are working to make this their *Best Year Ever! – and most importantly* – remind them about how much you love and believe in them! What a powerful way to end each day with your children while helping to prepare them for a great start to their next day!

Seven Winning Strategies

Winning Strategy 4
Attitude: Think Positive! Be Positive! Believe You Can Achieve!

"There is little difference in people, but that little difference makes a big difference. The little difference is <u>attitude</u>. The big difference is whether it is <u>positive</u> or <u>negative</u>."
~W. Clement Stone
Coauthor of Success Through A Positive Mental Attitude

"Passion is energy. Feel the power that comes from focusing on what excites you." ~Oprah Winfrey

"Belief is truly a magic word. It is the beginning of all success. It is the one quality you must develop before you can become a success." ~Napoleon Hill, Author of Think and Grow Rich

It is crucial that you help your children get in the practice of approaching each school day (and life in general) with a positive attitude, thinking positive thoughts, and looking for positive things to get excited and happy about. Remember, we tend to see more of what we focus on, so getting your children in the habit of looking for positive things to focus on will give them plenty of positive seeds (thoughts) to plant in their garden.

However, you can't stop there because *Attitude* is much more than just thinking positive thoughts. **It's also a lifestyle choice.**

Attitude is about learning to BE positive...living each day with passion, joy and a positive outlook expecting good things to happen. It's being someone that others enjoy working with and being around and being someone that takes on any and all challenges looking for solutions rather than excuses as to why they can't perform at their best.

Again, this is one of the main things employees can control in the workplace that will either help them to excel and thrive or cause them to barely survive and possibly get fired depending on their choice of attitude.

So, your goal this year is to help your children foster and grow a positive mindset that will help them to **think positive, be positive**, and **get them to believe they can achieve success!**

Note: Following is the continuation of the *Best Year Ever!* conversation **focusing on Attitude** – the second word in the three-word-success formula you want your children to master this year. Again, please don't feel you have to try and memorize and deliver this exact conversation. Use this to pull out key talking points you want to share with your children when talking about the importance of working to approach each day with a positive attitude and a strong belief in themselves.

Attitude

"The second thing in the three-word-success formula you need to do consistently this year in order to have your best year ever is to develop a strong, positive ATTITIUDE (or positive mindset). You must get in the habit of going to school each day looking for things to get excited and happy about, thinking positive thoughts, and expecting good things to happen.

Winning Strategy 4

SO MUCH OF OUR HAPPINESS DEPENDS ON HOW WE CHOOSE TO LOOK AT THE WORLD.

"*I want to tell you about a powerful cartoon (created by Genildo Ronchi) that really illustrates the difference between having a negative attitude and a positive attitude. It shows two men sitting across from each other on a bus. One man is slumped over in his seat, staring downward out his window, looking very sad and depressed. The other is sitting up straight in his seat, looking out his window with a big smile on his face, holding a camera in his hand as if he is anticipating taking some pictures. Above these two men in the cartoon is a caption that reads:* **'So much of our happiness depends on how we choose to look at the world.'**

"It's important for you to realize that both people in the cartoon are in the same place doing the same thing but are having two very different experiences because of their attitudes or mindsets. The one with the negative attitude seems to be having a miserable time. He is missing out on so many possible opportunities to see and experience some wonderful things because he has his head down and isn't looking for them.

"Meanwhile, the man with a positive attitude seems to be one hundred percent all in and having a great time. He is ready to take advantage of the opportunities he will have to see and experience many wonderful things. He has his head up and is looking for things to get excited and happy about. Plus, by holding up his camera, it is clear he expects/believes those opportunities will arise (see some amazing sites) and is prepared to take positive action (take pictures) when they do.

"I want you to realize that, like the bus riders in this cartoon, you get to determine if you want to have your best year ever or not based on which attitude and mindset you choose and what you decide to look for and do each day while you are at school.

"My hope is that you will be like the man on the bus that chose to have a positive mindset, and you will keep your head up with a smile on your face continually looking for things to get excited and happy about. I hope you, too, will believe and expect good things to happen and will always be prepared to take positive action when those opportunities arise.

"I want you to get in this same habit of thinking positive, being positive, and having a strong belief that you can achieve whatever you set your mind to accomplish this year – just like Michael Jordan **(or use the other successful person you chose earlier)** did each time he stepped out onto the basketball court believing he could make the big shots when needed. You, also, have to believe in yourself.

"The next time you think you won't be able to do something, keep this in mind: **If you want it badly enough, you'll find a way to get it**. I know this is true because I've seen each of you do this many times before. Just look at what all you were able to accomplish in the first five or six years of your lives! You learned how to walk, talk, read, and ride a bike as well as many other incredible things. Not one of these accomplishments were small. They were huge! And you did

Winning Strategy 4

them! You were able to accomplish these huge feats because you wanted to do them so badly you had no room in your brain for a negative mindset telling you that you're not good enough.

"You each had a strong desire to do these things, so you tapped into your natural positive attitude (mindset) to help you believe you could do them and then you went out and did them. That's the same attitude you'll need this year (and every year) to have your best year ever." **(To be continued)**

Note: Below Are Three **IDEAS/ACTIVITIES** Designed To Help Your Children Develop A Positive Attitude/Mindset:

🏃9: Place plenty of positive messages/quotes around your home that you want your children to think about. Place them in highly visible areas (on bathroom mirrors, the refrigerator, your children's bedroom walls, near clocks, etc.) and refer to them often whenever you can make any connections to the winning strategies and *success habits* mentioned in this book. Another idea you might want to consider is purchasing a small whiteboard and some dry erase markers that you can use to write the positive messages and quotes on you want your children to think about each day.

Be sure to change the positive quotes for new ones every week or two to help keep things interesting. Remember, you <u>must</u> be willing to model these quotes to help motivate your children to do the same. You will know these positive seeds are starting to take root when your children start referring to them and modeling them as well.

Note: To save time searching for quotes, use the ones I have included throughout this book, and go to my website (**bestyearever.net**) and download the PDF file of the collection of "Positive Quotes" on the *RESOURCES* page.

Seven Winning Strategies

**Here are several positive messages
you may want to use to help get started:**

- *Happiness is a choice.*
- *The way you choose to see the world creates the world you see.*
- *You are as smart as you choose to be.*
- *Believe you can achieve.*
- *Best Year Ever! – You have the Power to Make It Happen!*

🏃10: Start each morning (if possible) by sharing with your children three things you are excited and happy about or thankful for and quickly explain why. Next, have your children share their three things and why with you. The three things you each share can be big or little. It doesn't matter. What is important is to get your children focusing on positive things going on in their lives and to build the habit of being able to look for and identify the good things going on around them each day.

Make sure you all try to share three <u>new</u> things each day. You can even challenge each other to see how many days you can go in a row without repeating anything you've already shared before. By not repeating things they have shared, hopefully, your children will start to realize there are a lot of things to be happy and thankful for.

If you can't do this activity in the morning, try to find time after school to do this quick activity with your children – perhaps at dinner time or in the car on the way to or from an after school activity, or when you meet one-on-one with them each night to make sure they have everything needed for school the next day in place (see 🏃8). If you like, you can alter the activity by each sharing three things that went well at school/work that day that made you feel excited,

Winning Strategy 4

happy, proud or that you are grateful for and explain why for each.

To make this daily ritual even more impactful, you can each write your responses down in a little journal or notebook to keep track of and refer to often. Another idea to consider is for you all to write your responses on little slips of paper and put them in a large jar/vase which you can empty out onto a table once a week to review with your children. Both are a great way to help your children be able to see and remember all the wonderful things going on in your lives that make you all feel excited, happy, and grateful.

🏃11: The purpose of this activity is to motivate and help provide your children with some daily "nutritional food for thought" and to *target talk* positive things you want your children to think about and focus on. To get started, you will need to purchase some note cards. Start a collection of inspirational quotes that relate to the winning strategies and *success habits* mentioned in this book by writing one positive quote on each note card.

Note: To save time searching for quotes, go to my website (**bestyearever.net**) and download the PDF file of the collection of "Positive Quotes" on the *RESOURCES* page, and use the quotes throughout this book.

Every day, before school, give each child one of these positive, thought-provoking note cards. On the back of each card, be sure to write a quick message about what you think the quote means and how you think it pertains to them working to make this (and every year) their best year ever. Or, you can write some fun, personal notes that you think will make your children smile – giving them that little needed boost to help make their day even more positive.

Seven Winning Strategies

Don't forget to modify and adjust this activity to best fit each child's age, learning level, individual needs, and interests.

You may want to start each message with the following: ***"Welcome to Day #___*** (counting up the school days) ***of Your Best Year Ever!"*** And you might want to consider closing each note with the following: ***"Remember, Best Year Ever! You Have the Power to Make It Happen!"*** This will help give your children a daily reminder of the yearlong mindset/expectation/goal they are working on. It will also remind them that they have the power to reach this goal and do many other amazing things in life that's within their control if they so choose.

You can either hand it to each child on their way out the door each morning, or you can place the note cards in their lunch containers, backpacks, purses, or in anything else they carry to school with them each day. Make the cards easy to find because my guess is that once you give them a couple of these special note cards, your children will be expecting and looking forward to reading them each day, especially the personal notes you write on the back. By the way, these cards can possibly lead to some great follow up mini-discussions after school.

Winning Strategy 5
Effort: Try, Work Hard, and Don't Give Up!

"Genius is 1% talent and 99% hard work." ~Albert Einstein

"I've missed more than 9000 shots in my career. I've lost almost 300 games. 26 times, I've been trusted to take the game-winning shot and missed. I've failed over and over and over again in my life. And that is why I succeed."
~Michael Jordan

"It's hard to beat a person who never gives up." ~Babe Ruth

"The difference between ordinary and extraordinary is that little extra." ~Jimmy Johnson

One of the most valuable lessons or strategies you can teach your children to help them be successful, not just in school every year but throughout life in most everything they do and pursue, is to get them in the habit of rolling up their sleeves and be willing to put in the effort (work) it takes to succeed.

You need to convince your children that they can accomplish anything they set their mind to in life – if they are willing to show up on a regular basis with a positive, *can-do* attitude (growth mindset), are *willing to try* (to give effort), and keep trying until they get the results they want.

Seven Winning Strategies

You need to plant the seed in their minds that effort is all about trying...not trying to be perfect...but a strong desire to continue to give their best effort. Encourage your children to try and learn new things that will help them grow as students and people. Effort is about **learning to take risks and not being afraid to make mistakes. Mistakes will often provide them with opportunities to grow and succeed if they are willing to learn from them and not give up**.

Teach your children that perseverance pays. Most people that excel in school, work, and in life are those that are willing to give effort and keep giving effort until they get the results they want. Those that struggle or fail tend to be the ones who refuse to try (give effort) or give up too soon before they have given themselves enough time to succeed. **Therefore,** teach your children the value of sticking with things – especially when things get tough or seem to take longer than they hoped it would take to see the desired results.

Most importantly, help your children understand that effort is the difference between wishing for something and having the power to make it happen! The more **extra effort** they are willing to give, the more power they will have to make every school year (and beyond) their Best Year Ever! – and quite possibly **to take it from ordinary to extraordinary!**

Note: Following is the continuation of the *Best Year Ever!* conversation **focusing on Effort** – the third word in the three-word-success formula you want your children to master this year. Again, use this to pull out key talking points you want to share with your children about the importance of giving consistent effort – and extra effort whenever possible – to succeed at the things they set out to accomplish.

Winning Strategy 5

Effort

"The third thing you have to do this year in order to have your best year ever is to simply try. That's it, just try. You don't have to be perfect, just try. You have to give EFFORT, and you have to be willing to keep giving effort (working hard) until you get the results you want.

"Think about Michael Jordan **(or use the other successful person you chose earlier)**, even by showing up to play in each game with a positive, can-do attitude and a strong belief in himself, could not have succeeded in helping the Chicago Bulls win six NBA championships if he didn't give effort. When the whistle blew to start each game, he had to be willing to run, play defense, rebound, pass, and shoot the ball in order to help himself and his team be successful.

"It's important to note that as good as Michael Jordan was, he wasn't perfect. He made mistakes. He missed shots, made bad passes, and committed fouls in each and every game he played. However, he never let those mistakes stop him from trying to become the best player he could become. Instead, he used those mistakes to motivate himself to work even harder and get better by learning from them.

"To better explain the importance of getting in the habit of giving your best effort, I want to tell you about another extraordinary person. His name is Thomas Edison. He was an amazing inventor. Without Thomas Edison's effort, we would be sitting in the dark right now. We wouldn't have TV, movies, video games, and recordings of music to download and enjoy. He invented all these things – or their ancestors.

"Thomas Edison was able to invent many things because he wouldn't give up until he got the results he wanted. He wouldn't stop trying. His invention of the incandescent light bulb took more than 10,000 tries before he got it right. Ten thousand tries! Not ten tries or one hundred tries – more than 10,000 tries! To me, that's amazing! It also reminds me that if you really want something badly enough, and you don't quit trying, most likely you'll get it.

Seven Winning Strategies

"One last thing I want to tell you about Thomas Edison that made him so successful: Like Michael Jordan, he wasn't afraid to make mistakes. He didn't see mistakes as failures. He believed that making mistakes were necessary in order for learning to take place. He believed that each mistake brought him one step closer to reaching his goal. He believed failure occurred only if you didn't learn from your mistakes or when you quit trying too soon.

"Listen very closely to what I am about to tell you. It's something I want you to never forget the rest of your life. It's this…I don't expect you to be perfect. I'm telling you that it's okay to make mistakes this school year as long as you try to learn from them. Doesn't that feel good? No pressure! You don't have to be perfect. I also want you to know that this includes your teacher(s), classmates, friends, and family members – including me. No one is perfect, and everyone makes mistakes.

"However, all I ask and expect of you is that whenever you make a mistake you own up to it, tell the truth, and apologize when necessary. Always work to learn from each mistake so you don't keep repeating them. Just like I am asking you to do, I will do the same and work to learn from my mistakes and keep giving the effort to grow and improve as well.

"I have one more very important thing I want to share with you about effort. I want to let you in on a little secret about effort and success. People that tend to regularly put in **extra effort** – willing to do more than what's asked of them or willing to outwork those around them – tend to stand out and become quite successful at what they set out to accomplish, even if at first glance others doubted their abilities.

"When Michael Jordan first tried out for the high school varsity basketball team his sophomore year, he did not make the 15-man roster. Instead, he was placed on the junior varsity squad. He was considered too short (at the time) and wasn't deemed good enough yet to play at that level. As a child, Thomas Edison struggled in school and was labeled by

Winning Strategy 5

his teacher as being easily distracted and not very bright. However, both of these men became extraordinary individuals in their chosen professions…Why? Because they used these early setbacks in life to motivate them to outwork those around them and to give more than was expected of them. They got in the habit of always being willing to give extra effort!!

"So the next time you're wrestling with a math problem or don't understand what your teacher is trying to teach you, relax and think about Michael Jordan and his six NBA championships and Thomas Edison and the light bulb and all his other amazing inventions. **Keep trying, don't give up, and get in the habit of giving extra effort** *whenever possible – because you may only be one mistake or one more try away from success and quite possibly doing something extraordinary with your life.*

"That's it. Attendance, Attitude, and Effort! Master these three words this year and I promise you'll have a year to remember…your best year ever!"

Note: This concludes the *Best Year Ever!* mindset/vision/goal conversation.

🚶12: Place more focus and appreciation on your children's *effort* and *learning* this school year rather than on *results* – trusting that the desired results will come.

Each morning, remind your children to have fun and to give their best effort at school that day. Get in the habit of asking them, each day after school, more about *what* they are currently learning or something specific they learned that day instead of asking only about grades they are getting on assignments, tests, and projects. Put more emphasis and value on **effort** and **growth vs. results** to help motivate them to continue to give their best effort as they work to build a strong growth mindset this school year.

Seven Winning Strategies

Yes, *results* (test scores, grades, and report cards/evaluations) are very important in school and life! However, by putting more emphasis on helping your children build a positive, growth mindset rather than just focusing on results, you will help eliminate a lot of the performance pressure that many students (especially those with a fixed mindset) often feel. *By doing this, it will help increase your children's joy of learning, engagement in what they are learning, and the effort that leads to better results*!

Like the gardener planting seeds, be patient. Give this time and remain confident that the results will come!

When your children start bringing home news of better results (which they will) on tests, assignments, and projects, instead of praising them for being "so smart" or "talented," plant the seeds that let them know how proud you are about the amount of **time**, **energy**, and **effort** they are putting into their work to get those results. Again, this will motivate and encourage your children to continue working hard and trying new things. This will most likely lead to even better results throughout this school year and beyond.

🏃13: Another great message to share with your children at the start of every school year is to remind them that this is a new school year – a fresh start. To help deliver this important message, share with them the following quote: ***"Your past doesn't equal your future."*** Explain that this school year is a new beginning. Remind your children that if they have had great years in the past, this can be another great year. However, if they have struggled in the past, this is the chance to start fresh as a student that does well and enjoys going to school.

This school year is a great time to reinforce to your children that you won't compare them to their siblings or other kids because you are only interested in giving them a chance to define who *they* are and to be themselves. Let them know that you hope they won't waste their time comparing themselves to others but instead, will focus more on all their good traits as they continue to strive to be the best they can be. It's not a competition against anyone else. It's more about learning to expect the best, working to make it happen, and enjoying themselves as they go forward.

Here is another thing worth noting with regards to making a fresh start. You want to constantly be reminding your children that they have an opportunity to make each day, each hour of every day, and each moment a fresh start – especially when they have made a mistake, have had a bad day, or seem to be struggling or in a slump. **Encourage them to shake it off, relax, start fresh with a positive attitude, keep giving their best effort and have fun doing it!**

Seven Winning Strategies

Winning Strategy 6

Become a Goal Setter and Goal-Getter by Following These Six Steps

"A life without dreams is like a garden without flowers."
~Author Unknown

"The biggest adventure you can ever take is to live the life of your dreams." ~Oprah Winfrey

"It's a dream until you write it down. Then it's a goal." ~Emmitt Smith

"Our goals can only be reached through a vehicle of a plan, in which we must fervently believe, and upon which we must vigorously act. There is no other route to success." ~Pablo Picasso

The quote by C. S. Lewis, "You are never too old to set another goal or to dream a new dream," is so true. However, when it comes to your children, it is also important to note that **you are never too young to start dreaming big dreams and setting exciting goals**. Because a life without dreams would truly be like a garden without flowers – a life void of passion.

To help ensure that your children are learning to *grow beautiful flowers in their garden* you want them to start dreaming big dreams and working to achieve clearly defined goals. This will provide them with a positive perspective that they are living their lives with purpose and direction and will help create a great sense of accomplishment each time they achieve a goal by making one of their dreams come true!

Allow your children to dream big dreams. By all means, try to avoid shooting down any of their dreams (as far-fetched as they may seem to be). *Don't pluck out those seeds before they have a chance to take root and start to grow.* Instead, get excited about your children's dreams and tell them you are looking forward to working with them to help come up with a solid game plan to help achieve those dreams. This will also send a strong message that you believe in them. Then, as you work through the six-step process listed below, you can help break their really big goals down into smaller bite-sized goals or action steps that will lead toward their larger goals.

So, now that you are well on your way to helping your children develop a strong, positive *can-do* attitude and have provided them with the three-word-success formula to help make this (and every year) their *Best Year Ever!*, it's time to **give your children a definite plan** that will allow them to grow *many beautiful flowers in their gardens* for years to come – living their lives with passion and purpose.

Note: Follow this six-step plan throughout the school year to help your children learn how to become successful goal setters and goal-getters.

1. BELIEVE YOU CAN ACHIEVE: Having a growth mindset seems to introduce any success story. It is the foundation on which everything else should be built. It is believing that you can do anything if you are willing to work for it.

Winning Strategy 6

It is also about having a positive mindset – being able to use your brain like a computer that you program to help search for things to get excited and happy about. Like a gardener, you learn to weed out the bad, self-defeating thoughts, and plant the positive thoughts you want to grow.

Being able to visualize yourself already successful at whatever you want to accomplish is a valuable skill that many successful people have mastered.

2. SET CLEAR GOALS: It is the road map that leads to success. It's the target on which you set your sights and focus your energy. Studies show that people who set goals tend to have more success in life than those that don't. **Those that set goals *and* take the time to write them down, tend to be more successful** than those that set goals but don't write them down. Therefore, get in the habit of taking time **every day** (if possible) to write down your goals and any new ones that come to mind no matter how far-fetched they may seem. When you do this, write them as if you have already achieved them.

For example, change goals like "I will try to miss less school this year" to "*I have great attendance and almost never miss any school!*"…"I will try not to mess around at school as much" to "*I am a strong leader and role model in my classroom and on the playground!*"…"I will try to do better at my cross country meets" to "*I am running faster at each meet and shaving time off my best time!*"…"I will try to learn my multiplication facts" to "*I know all my multiplication facts which makes doing math much easier and more fun!*"…"I will try not to get so nervous playing my saxophone at our concerts" to "*I enjoy playing my saxophone with confidence at our concerts, and I sound great!*"

If you want, you can even take this a step further. Post your written goals somewhere so you can look at them often. **Writing down your goals and posting** them where you can constantly see and read them will have a much more powerful effect than just trying to remember them.

The key is to decide what exciting things you want to do and achieve. If you like, start by setting smaller goals first then working up to larger ones as you gain more confidence in your ability to achieve the goals you set. To give yourself an even better chance of reaching your goals, **create a game plan** you can follow by writing down all the *action steps* (things you need to do) in order to hit the target you want to hit.

3. TAKE ACTION: Once you set your goals and have them written down (including the action steps you will take), it is time to start working on them. For example, you can map out a beautiful, detailed plan to create the most wonderful day, but unless you get out of bed, get dressed and get going, you will have missed the opportunity to make that wonderful day a reality. You cannot just desire it or plan for it, you have to **take action based on your plan to make it work**. This is the difference between wishing for something and making it happen!

Approach the process of taking action like learning to run. You first have to learn to crawl, walk, and jog before you can run. Don't try to climb the mountain in one leap. Take each action step one step at a time leading toward your goal until you finally reach it.

4. MONITOR AND ADJUST: You have to look up every once in a while and see whether you are still moving toward your target. If not, you have to be willing to change what you're doing to get back on track. You have to look at problems as opportunities to grow and mistakes as a chance to learn.

5. PERSEVERANCE: This is where you have to adopt Thomas Edison's ability to stick with things long enough to get the results you want. Remember, it took him more than 10,000 tries to invent the incandescent light bulb. Don't quit too soon! Push yourself to keep going.

6. REPETITION: Redo steps one to five over-and-over again! This is the glue that will make it stick and eventually become a positive habit that you will have to use to your advantage for the rest of your life. Each of these steps will start to become second nature with enough practice and repetition.

Note: Following Are Three **IDEAS/ACTIVITIES** Designed To Help Your Children Practice Becoming Goal Setters and Goal-Getters:

🕺14: To help jumpstart your children into becoming goal setters and goal-getters, get them each a little notebook where they can write down their big dreams, personal goals, action steps, and updates on the goals they decide to work on throughout the school year. In fact, you should get

Seven Winning Strategies

one for yourself as well, so you can model to them throughout the year how you, too, are a goal setter and goal-getter.

Before starting to set specific goals to start working on (see 🏃15), tell your children that the first thing you are each going to work on is brainstorming (creating) a list of long and short term dreams and goals you each individually (or together) would like to achieve. Depending on each child's age, you can work with them to help create their list or they can work on their own. Tell them that their goals can be both school-related and not related to school. Again, depending on each child's age, you can have them try to create a list of at least 5-10 (or more) goals with you doing the same. Once your lists are complete you can share them with each other and start deciding which goals you would each like to work on first.

🏃15: At the start of every month you each choose one of the short term goals that you would like to achieve by the end of the month. This activity is designed to show your children the power of writing down a goal and taking time each day to focus on that goal to increase their odds of achieving it. This approach can also be used when working to achieve larger, long-term goals.

Steps to follow:

1. Ask each child to think of a goal they'd like to accomplish by the end of the month. Think of a goal that you will work on as well. Make sure everyone's goals are realistic for this time frame and are something they really want to accomplish.

2. Have each child use the following formula to write out their goal in their goal notebook and on an index card they can post someplace in their bedroom:

Winning Strategy 6

Write the goal as if you've already achieved it, a time limit to reach your goal, what you'll be doing to reach your goal (action steps) – trying to keep it to 25 words or less.

Example of a Goal: *I memorized all my multiplication facts in four weeks by practicing doing flashcards with my parent(s) ten minutes per night.*

3. Meet individually with each child every day (possibly during the same time you meet together for 🏃8). Take two minutes to each **rewrite** the goal you are working on that month in your goal notebooks. You can also both use this time to visualize your own goal as if it's already been accomplished and what you're doing to accomplish it.

4. Then ask each other if you think you are on track to reach your goal by the end of the month. Discuss how it's going. Use this time to encourage each other to keep going and to work together to problem-solve any issues either of you may be having with your goal.

5. At the end of the month, check to see how you both did in reaching your own goal. Take a few minutes to explain to each other why you did/didn't accomplish it and how you feel about reaching/not reaching your goal. Then, write about it in your goal notebooks. If your child reached their goal, be sure to **celebrate and praise them for their effort** to make their goal a reality. If they did not reach their goal but decide to continue working on it, **praise them for their perseverance**.

6. Set new goals (or continue working on a previous goal that needs more time to be achieved) for the upcoming month and repeat the process.

Note: By taking the time and making the effort to participate in this activity with your children, you are modeling to them that you think this is something worth doing. Also, by sharing with your children at the end of the month if you were able/unable to achieve your goal, you get to share what helped or hindered you. This will create a great teachable moment as they continue to become goal setters and goal-getters.

🏃**16**: One goal you need to set that will have the biggest impact on your children throughout their schooling and beyond is to help them get in the habit of reading (or being read to at a young age) at least 20 minutes every day. There have been countless studies done on the benefits kids gain by reading daily outside of school compared to those who don't. **Besides building their vocabulary and reading and writing skills** – *that will lead to more academic success* – it will open up many new worlds to them, help develop their imagination, and will build their self-confidence. The list of benefits is endless!

Seriously, I cannot begin to emphasize enough what a huge game changer this will be in your children's lives if you can get them to read for at least 20 minutes a day.

However, for many kids, it's hard to find an extra twenty minutes a day outside of school to read. There is a lot of competition already out there fighting for their time including participating in after school activities, completing homework and chores, wanting to play with friends, playing video games, watching television, etc. So here is a plan to create a daily twenty-minute window where they won't see it as some kind of punishment taking them away from what they would rather be doing.

To start, you need to make a deal with your children where you will *allow* them to stay up twenty minutes past their bedtime each night to read in bed. The only stipulations are that at the end of the twenty minutes they will not be allowed to get out of bed, so they must take care of all their needs before they start to read. Also, they must read from a book rather than an electronic device with a screen. Studies show that using electronic devices close to bedtime can make it more difficult to go to sleep and stay asleep. If your children are too young to read on their own, read a book to them for 20 minutes.

Be sure to allow your children to pick a book that will hold their interest and be enjoyable to read – preferably a good chapter book. Don't worry if you don't have a lot of books available at home because your kids will most likely be able to borrow a book from their classroom or check one out from the school or your local public library.

Remember, the goal is to make this reading time as enjoyable as possible to help get them in the habit of wanting to read every day.

Seven Winning Strategies

Winning Strategy 7

Consistently Use a Team Approach and Strive to Become a Strong Team Player

"When spider webs unite, they can tie up a lion."
~*Ethiopian proverb*

"Remember no one succeeds alone.
Never walk alone in your future paths."
~*Sonia Sotomayor, Associate Justice of the Supreme Court*
of the United States

"Talent wins games, but teamwork and intelligence
win championships." ~*Michael Jordan*

"We rise by lifting others." ~*Robert G. Ingersoll*

I have saved this powerful, winning strategy for last because I feel it is important to never forget that to achieve any goal or level of success (individually, as a group, or as a team) you will always need the help and support of others.

As talented as Michael Jordan was, he never could have won any of the Bulls' six NBA championships without the help of his fellow players, coaches, trainers, and many others. The same will be true for your children every year in school and throughout their entire lives. Not only will they need your help and support (like I mentioned earlier: *YOU are their primary and most influential role model, teacher, and coach*), they will also need the help and support of countless others throughout their lives helping them make this and every year in school (and beyond) their *Best Year Ever!*

Therefore, you must impress upon your children the importance of learning to consistently use a team approach when working with others to accomplish individual and/or shared goals and to be strong team players (good teammates)!

Think about how important this is. Think about how many different times and situations your children will be asked or expected to work with others to complete a job, collective mission, or goal in their lifetimes. Not to master this strategy, no matter how well they master the other six winning strategies, will most definitely hold each back from reaching their full potential and enjoying the sense of belonging and accomplishment that comes when you join forces with others to make things happen!

Reinforce to your children that you are a team working together to help make this their *Best Year Ever!* Let them know that as their teammate/coach, you are totally committed to giving them your absolute best effort to help make it happen. Also, let your children know that they can rely on you to help encourage them, cheer them on, be there to help *them* solve any problems or challenges they may face, and will celebrate their accomplishments with them throughout the year.

Finally, explain to your children that you look forward to working closely and cooperatively with their teacher(s) as teammates this year to help them have their *Best Year Ever!* – and that you expect them to do the same with their teacher(s) and classmates.

Winning Strategy 7

Challenge your children to go to school each day working to become a strong team player and leader by modeling to their teacher(s) and classmates the following traits:

- **Being Coachable:** Be able and willing to do the things you are being asked to do and make the suggested adjustments needed to improve or help the team.

- **Reliable and Responsible:** Teacher(s) and students can depend on you to show up each day on time, with a positive, *can-do* attitude, follow the rules, and complete and turn in work on time.

- **Take Initiative:** Be someone that takes action without having to be asked or told to do something that needs to be done.

- **Can Be Trusted:** You are honest, trustworthy, and do the right thing even when no one is watching.

- **Respectful and Supportive:** You accept everyone by not putting others down with your words or actions. Help those in need, encourage teammates, and look for opportunities to help/serve others – like your teacher(s) and classmates, and other children and adults in your school.

- **Positive and Enthusiastic:** You consistently display a pleasing, upbeat, optimistic personality looking for and expecting good things to happen.

- **Problem Solver:** Instead of causing problems, you are good at helping to solve problems and look for positive solutions to help individuals and the team improve and grow.

Seven Winning Strategies

- **Accountable:** You hold yourself accountable/responsible for your behavior and don't try to cover up or blame others when you make mistakes. Instead, you own your mistakes (tell the truth), apologize when necessary, and learn from your mistakes so you don't keep repeating them.
- **Lead By Example:** You understand that actions speak louder than words so you try to show others what to do by your actions – you model the way.
- **Give Extra Effort:** You get in the habit of doing more than what is asked or expected of you to do whenever possible.

Share with your children that the **more traits listed above they can master** and get in the habit of using throughout their lives, **the more they will be successful and stand out as strong team players and leaders**. It is important to let your children know that each of these traits can be attained by anyone that has a desire to learn them and is willing to put forth the effort to achieve them. Let each child know that you understand all this sounds like a lot more work and effort on their part – especially at first. However, over time, the benefits of being seen and respected as a strong teammate and leader will be highly valued in many areas of their life throughout their lifetime.

Finally, one of the most valuable lessons you can teach your children to help make every year in school (and beyond) their *Best Year Ever!* is to **get them in the habit of trying to be positive role models who are always looking for opportunities to serve others**, who will reach out and help those around them when they see the need. Not only will it help to uplift and empower those they serve, but it will also help to uplift and empower them. It won't take long for your children to realize, like a boomerang, the more joy and support they give to others, the more it will come back to them as well.

Note: The final four **IDEAS/ACTIVITIES** are designed to help you help your children master the powerful leadership traits mentioned above as well as providing your children and you plenty of positive things to talk about throughout the entire school year (and beyond) – keeping them focused on the seven winning strategies.

🏃17: Choose one of the leadership traits listed on the two previous pages (or one of the seven winning strategies). Make it a **"Success Skill of the Week"** that you will *target talk* with your children encouraging them to focus on and practice using each day at school throughout the week. You can even write a little daily reminder to them on their daily note cards (see 🏃11) to look for opportunities to use that skill at school that day.

Each evening when you are checking in with them to make sure they have everything in place they'll need for school the next day (see 🏃8), you can ask each child how they practiced using that skill during school that day – praising them for their effort and offering suggestions of how they can use it the next day. Be sure to share with your children examples of how you are using that same skill each day during the week to help model the way.

🏃18: Here is a quick, daily activity you can do to send a strong message to your children to go into school each day looking for opportunities to help/serve others while working to make this year their *Best Year Ever!*

Get in the habit of asking your children at least one of the following five questions every day after school:

- What was one thing you did today to help your teacher?
- What did you do today to help out a classmate?
- What did you do today to help make your school a little better?
- What did you do today to help make this year your best year ever?
- What did you do today to help yourself?

When you like what you hear, be sure to praise them and let them know you are proud of them for making the effort to be positive role models. **Your sincere praise will encourage them to repeat this behavior.**

🏃19: Encourage your children to go out into the world each day trying to represent themselves, your family, and your family name well with their words and actions. This will hopefully help to motivate them to make good choices at school each day. It is important for your children to learn early and often that the choices they make not only can have positive or negative effects on them but others as well – like your family, their classmates, any teams they play on, or groups they are associated with.

To help your children realize this, provide them with many examples of things you do daily to help represent yourself, your family, and family name well (or the company/organization you work for and/or your profession) by your words and actions. This awareness may very well discourage them from making poor choices because they want to be more like you by trying not to let others down.

Again, be sure to praise and let your children know how proud you are of them, and even thank them for the times they make the effort to represent themselves, your family, and your family name well with their words and actions.

Winning Strategy 7

🚶20: Find as many opportunities as you can to *target talk* or casually work into the conversation the positive things you want your children to think about and focus on that will help uplift and empower them at school and in all areas of their lives. Like a gardener, your goal is to keep planting seeds (positive thoughts and belief in self) while plucking out any weeds (negative thoughts and self-doubt) that could hold them back from growing.

Instead of lecturing them, or trying to drill into them, the importance of working to master the seven winning strategies including the three-word-success formula (**attendance**, **attitude**, **effort**), find ways you can purposely (but casually) work these winning strategies and success habits into your regular conversations and daily interactions with them.

Note: Below are three topics of conversation you can use throughout the school year to accomplish this goal.

Topic #1

Start sharing "success stories" with your children that will help inspire them. Give them plenty of real-life examples of how others have overcome setbacks in their lives and/or accomplished something special by dreaming big dreams and then working to make them happen by using many of the seven winning strategies discussed in this book.

Go to your public library and search in the biography section or search online to find true stories about real people throughout history (deceased or currently living) who were able to accomplish something special in their lives. This list can include famous athletes, business people, civic leaders, civil rights leaders, government officials, entertainers, etc.

Start collecting success stories about these people that you can <u>read</u>, <u>show</u>, and <u>tell</u> your children about. Take a few minutes after each story to ask your children which of the winning strategies or words from their three-word-success formula they feel each person used and mastered in order to become successful. Next, have them explain their answers. Remind them that they have the same power within to make their dreams come true once they master and consistently use the same strategies.

It's important to emphasize that these people were not born lucky or suddenly got lucky; rather, they had to work hard and persevere to make their luck happen. You'll discover that, in many cases, the people you learn about came from less-than-ideal situations. It's important for your children to realize that they'll empower themselves so much more when *they* decide to make their own luck happen by using these winning strategies instead of waiting around for luck to find them.

Topic #2

Tell your children success stories from your own life and people you personally know (including your children) where you/they have accomplished special things and overcame specific challenges. These stories may very likely have a bigger impact on them because they have happened to people close to home who they can really connect with. Be sure to **follow the same steps in Topic #1** when telling and discussing these success stories with your children – especially when the success stories are about them. What a powerful way to remind them that they have already been successful using a lot of these winning strategies without even realizing it.

Topic #3

Always be on the lookout in your day-to-day activities for opportunities to make connections to people using the seven winning strategies that you can share with your children. For example, you may be reading or discussing a book with them or watching a TV show, movie, or ballgame on television and notice that one of the characters or athletes seems to be doing really well. Or maybe, you are out and about with your children shopping or eating at a restaurant, and you come across someone who is providing excellent service. Or quite possibly, you may come across situations where they will start telling you about how well something went for them at school or in other areas in their lives.

All of these situations (and countless others) will provide you with great examples and opportunities to *target talk* and highlight the positive things you want your children to think about and focus on. Better yet, ask your children to identify and share with you the winning strategies or *success habits* each of the people in these situations were using. It can lead to some great mini-discussions about the importance of the following traits:

Having a Growth Mindset
Showing Up On a Regular Basis
Thinking Positive Thoughts
Believing In Yourself
Living With Passion and Purpose
Consistently Giving Your Best Effort
Not Giving Up
Becoming a Goal Setter and Goal-Getter
Working Well With Others
Being a Strong Role Model and Leader
Working to Make Every Year Your Best Year Ever!

Closing Thoughts

"Some people want it to happen, some wish it would happen, others make it happen." ~Michael Jordan

Well, there you have it, the seven winning strategies (and twenty IDEAS/ACTIVITIES) you can use to help your children thrive and prosper. **Remember,** these strategies will work like magic if you consistently model the way, talk daily with your children about the power of thinking positive thoughts and dreaming big dreams. Help your children use each strategy long enough to start seeing positive results. **Most importantly,** have fun working together with your children – and their school(s) throughout the year.

I was motivated to write this book and share these seven winning strategies with you because I know as a parent and former teacher, you want your children to be successful and happy at school each year and throughout their lives. I, too, want your children (and all children) to be successful and happy. Therefore, my hope is that by using this book, I will be able to help you do just that with your children! Also, *I hope that you will take the time to share this powerful little book with others* – family members and friends whose children you think will benefit from using these seven winning strategies.

In closing, as you work with your children using this book, I hope you will always remember that one of the true marks of success and living a life with joy and purpose is best summed up by a quote from Gregory Scott Reid:

*"The greatest success we'll know
is helping others succeed and grow."*

Seven Winning Strategies

By teaching your children to try and live by this quote every day, and by helping them to master these seven winning strategies, you will have provided them with many of the *success habits* and tools they will need to help make this and every year in school (and beyond) their ***Best Year Ever!***

I want to wish you all the best as you work to make this *the greatest success you'll know by helping your children succeed and grow.* Always remember, you (and your children) have the power to **MAKE IT HAPPEN!**

Message to Schools, School Districts, and PTO/PTA

My goal is for you to be able to Give a Free Copy of *Seven Winning Strategies* **to the parents of all your students**, providing them with seven powerful strategies (and twenty IDEAS/ACTIVITIES) they can use to help their children develop strong *success habits* to succeed every year in school and throughout their lives. I want you to be able to do this **AT NO COST TO YOUR SCHOOL/DISTRICT!**

In order to accomplish this, all you need to do is *enlist the help of your PTO/PTA to sponsor or recruit local businesses to become a proud sponsor of your school/district by purchasing the books for your parents*. Not only will they be able to *purchase the books in packs of 50 copies at 50% off the cover price* (plus shipping and handling), but they will also have a sticker with their business name and contact information placed inside the back cover of each book next to the heading: ***Please Thank and Support Our Generous Sponsor(s)***. Your school/district will provide the sticker(s).

For more information or to purchase *Seven Winning Strategies* go to **bestyearever.net**. You can also contact me by email (billcecil@bestyearever.net) or by phone (517-244-0465) to find out more about my availability to speak or conduct workshops with your parents, students, and teachers.

Message to Local Businesses and Other Potential Sponsors

Please consider helping a local school/district in your community to be able to **GIVE A FREE COPY** of *Seven Winning Strategies* **to the parents of their students**. By doing so, you will be providing them with seven powerful strategies (and twenty IDEAS/ACTIVITIES) they can use to help their children develop strong *success habits* to succeed every year in school and throughout their lives. What a great way to give back to many of the families and educators that support and frequent your business!

Becoming a proud sponsor by purchasing these books is not only a great way to make a goodwill gesture within your community but also **makes good business sense**. As a sponsor, you will be able to *purchase the books in packs of 50 copies at 50% off the cover price* (plus shipping and handling), and you will also have a sticker with your business name and contact information placed inside the back cover of each book next to the heading: *Please Thank and Support Our Generous Sponsor(s)*. The school/district will provide the sticker(s).

Below are just some of the many other benefits of sponsorship to consider:

- A great way to strengthen your business image
- An effective and affordable way to advertise locally
- A guaranteed way to reach people in your community looking for your service/product
- Increased business and referrals
- People are more likely to support those businesses that support the local schools

For more information or to purchase *Seven Winning Strategies* go to **bestyearever.net** or contact me by email (billcecil@bestyearever.net) or by phone (517-244-0465).

BEST YEAR EVER!

Providing Positive Products to Help Make It Happen!

Visit us @ BestYearEver.net

Please Thank and Support Our Generous Sponsor(s)